More Old BLAIRGOWRIE and R

by
Maurice Fleming

A steam engine calls at Holmrigg, Essendy, to collect freshly picked raspberries. The engine took the barrels to Blairgowrie Railway Station for despatch to markets in the south. An engine such as this would have been quite an advance on the slower horse and cart. Raspberries were first grown locally in 1890 and the industry took off with the founding of a fruitgrowers' association three years later.

ISBN 1 84033 252 2

FURTHER READING

The books listed below were used by the author during his research. None are available from Stenlake Publishing. Those interested in finding out more are advised to contact their local bookshop or reference library.

Anon., *Rattray an' its Fowk*.
Peter Dawson, *Mills on the Ericht* (thesis), 1950.
Nick Haynes, *Perth & Kinross: An Illustrated Architectural Guide*, 2000.
John A.R. MacDonald, *The History of Blairgowrie*, 1899.
Adam Malcolm, *Our Heritage Walks* (series), 1994.
D. Moody (ed.), *Old Blairgowrie*, 1976.
The *Blairgowrie Advertiser* (newspaper files).

ACKNOWLEDGEMENTS

While most of the pictures published here are from my own collection, I am also extremely grateful to the following who have either lent pictures or provided information: Bill Baird, Shirley Campbell, Douglas and Graeme Davidson, Frank Davidson, John Dow, William Heron, the late Adam Malcolm, Eric Grant, Irene Morrison, Pat McGregor, Marr Paterson, David M. Phillips, James Sloggie, Marjory Ross, David Scott, Myra Shearer, Bessie Smith, Jennifer Woods, Denholm Reid and Bobbie Sommerville. My thanks also to Jane Higgins for her computing skills.

Built in 1852 on the site of an earlier townhouse, the Royal Hotel occupies a commanding position at the Cross, looking along the length of the High Street. Although horsepower is to the fore in this scene, the sign for the 'Motor Garage' at the top of the building was a portent of things to come. The name of the Fairs family, who owned the hotel for many years, is above the door.

Keiller's Restaurant, right, was a popular venue for a number of years. In this photograph from 1955 there is an intriguing glimpse, in the gap between the Post Office and the Royal Hotel, of the old house that was demolished to make a car and coach park.

Some years before the present traffic flow system was introduced, these islands were seen as the answer to relieve Blairgowrie's High Street congestion. Many will have fond memories of the businesses on the left – McQuattie's 'Swete Shoppe', Ward's the stationer's, and McLeish's fish shop. On the right are D. & H. Birse, Fleming the grocer's and Mr Black's beautifully appointed chemist's. All of these businesses are gone.

Names to remember – J. & A. Reid's was a popular downtown grocer's and baker's at No. 5 Leslie Street. This is now a hardware and ironmongery store.

Alex Petrie at No. 23 High Street was a well patronised grocer, wine merchant and 'Italian Warehouseman'. The clock is one feature that has survived in the many changes on the High Street, although these premises have been a restaurant for some years.

Gunn's Hotel, left, boasted that it was 'patronised by the elite' and had 'over 30 well-appointed apartments'. It promised that 'omnibuses and porters' would meet all trains and that a 'motor char-a-banc' bound for Braemar departed from the hotel at 3 p.m. daily. The building now contains several flats. Did the dog move out of the way to allow the car up Brown Street?

Local boy scouts on their way to church in the mid-1930s. They marched from the Malt Barns at the top of Kirk Wynd to the South Church on Reform Street. This was their pipe band's first public appearance and they could play only one tune, 'The Earl of Mansfield'. By this point Douglas Neil, on the right, had lost his hat which had blown off! The shop in the background, overlooking the Cross, belonged to J.B. McGibbon, ironmonger and seedsman.

A bill head from a Victorian predecessor of J.B. McGibbon.

In this view a selection of shops lines both sides of the High Street and flags fly bravely from the Queen's and Royal Hotels. Adamson's ironmongery, right, was on two floors and carried a wide stock of goods.

Trees and bollards featured in the Wellmeadow of the early 1920s. A drinking trough for horses can be seen on the left. Opposite it, at the foot of the telegraph pole, is the town weigh-house. Loads of farm or other products were weighed on the platform alongside and the controls in the hut were worked by a weighman operating a horizontal bar and weights. Notice the simple exterior of the then modestly sized Angus Hotel on the right.

The Commercial Bank of Scotland is one of several bank branches to have come and gone in the town over the years. This 1951 photograph was taken at a time when the Wellmeadow still presented no great problems for motorists, cyclists or pedestrians.

A cattle sale, open air market and fun fair all rolled into one, the Fair o' Blair used to be the highlight of the town's year. Traditionally centred on the Wellmeadow, which was then an open space, it attracted huge crowds. It was held every 23 July until 1890, after which it was switched to the last Tuesday of that month. The Macpherson Memorial Fountain, left, was erected in 1893 in memory of Allan Macpherson, local laird and Deputy Lieutenant of the County.

Charlie Smith's truck, with Britannia on board, at Rattray Common on the day of King George V's Silver Jubilee celebrations in 1935. Charlie was a grain and coal merchant with an office in Tannage Street. His vehicles were always as immaculate as this. Despite his family's protests he used to spend every Saturday afternoon washing and polishing them!

The Silver Jubilee procession passes down the Wellmeadow. The banner 'Long Live their Majesties' is on Fleming the draper's shop.

Standing or walking on the streets is a luxury we can no longer enjoy and this is a reminder of more peaceful times. Johnny Small's barber's pole can be seen next to 'Po' Craig's china shop. Note the elegant lamps on either side of the bridge and beside Nellie Marshall's shop doorway on the right.

The photograph of Newton Street was taken before the garage of John Harper and Sons extended to take in more ground on the right-hand side. Harper's, founded in 1890 as a blacksmith's and general engineer's, grew to become the pioneers of motoring in Blairgowrie.

Snow scenes were a favourite subject of postcard producers early last century. This one looks south along the stretch of Perth Road between the top of Dunkeld Road and the point in the distance where it is joined by Shaw Street. Unfortunately there is no clue on the card to identify either the photographer or the year of this particular snowfall.

Today the name Rosemount is used to cover an ever widening area on the outskirts of Blairgowrie. This card shows the heart of the original hamlet. The group of cottages strung along Coupar Angus Road includes the leafy post office which served the villagers.

Walkers have long enjoyed the views over the town from Burnhead Road. The views remain, but this rough track has since become a proper road with houses along its upper side.

"RECORD FLOOD AT BLAIRGOWRIE. 29-8-10."

When the River Ericht rose to an impressive height in August 1910, the enterprising local newspaperman D.G. Monair was there to photograph the scene and rush it out as a postcard. It was a scoop typical of the Irish-born Monair and if he retouched the swell on the waters a little to make the river look even more turbulent, who would complain? The photograph became one of the town's best known images.

This postcard was posted in 1904 and it is a long time since cattle grazed by the Ericht within sight of the Brig o' Blair. The Methodist Church, left, was built in 1887 thanks to a surprise legacy left to the congregation by a member of another denomination in the town. One arch of the 1777 bridge was swept away in a flood in the autumn of 1847, but it was speedily rebuilt.

The King's Visit to Blairgowrie,
September 1908
Waiting for His Majesty

The town was elaborately decorated on 28 September, 1908, when King Edward VII arrived by car from Balmoral. After his visit he boarded the royal train at the railway station, bound for an engagement at Dunblane. This was the scene at the bridge on that very wet, dreich, day.

"UNION IS STRENGTH."

Mount Ericht and South Church,
.. Blairgowrie ..

"One in Mine Hand."—Ezek. xxxvii. 19.
16th August, 1906.

From Photos by J. D. Petrie.

First Entry in Session Records, 26th May, 1757.

Rattray—John Henderson, 1762-1789.
Thomas Wood, - 1793-1810.
James Aird, - - 1812-1834.

David Hogg, - 1835-1837.
John Paterson, 1839-1844.
Robert Russell, 1847-1897.
David Arnot, M.A., 1895.

South Church { Robert Taylor, M.A., 1858-1864.
Chas. G. McCrie, D.D., 1865-1873.
Malcolm White, M.A., 1874-1906.

A card issued to mark the linking of two local United Free churches in 1906. Rattray's Mount Ericht closed that year and the congregation moved across the river to the South Church, right. Mount Ericht, now divided into flats, opened in 1835 and the South in 1858. The first company of the Boys' Brigade in the town was formed at Mount Ericht.

From the looks of these faces, working for Blairgowrie Post Office at the start of last century was a deadly serious business. The group includes counter staff, postmen and telegraph boys, one with his bicycle. The building seen here is No. 1 High Street which the post office occupied for many years. Prior to that it was based at other premises in the High Street (two different addresses) and Allan Street. It has since been on its travels again and is now within a supermarket.

Alex Steven, centre, with his staff outside his barber's shop at No. 16 Allan Street around 1920. Mr Steven's grand manner when wielding a razor was watched with awe by small boys waiting for a haircut. The premises remained a hairdresser's under other proprietors for some years, but has been the Bookshop since 2000.

A line-up of staff outside Wm Stewart Ltd, Nos. 31–33 Leslie Street, in 1931. Third from the left is Charlie Clark who was to become the shop's last proprietor. The left-hand part of the premises sold fish while the other half was devoted to high class groceries, including a wide range of wines and spirits.

24

Once a common sight in harvest fields at home and abroad, the Bisset Binder was devised and made in Greenbank Works, Dunkeld Road. The company was started in 1835 by Thomas Bisset who began his working life as a blacksmith at Marlee. Other agricultural machines were also produced at Greenbank to Bisset's specifications and in its heyday the foundry employed a large work force. It shut down in the 1960s and the A. Proctor Group has since found a new industrial use for the site.

Walter Davidson, photographed outside his Wellmeadow chemist's shop when he stood for re-election to Blairgowrie Town Council in 1926. He was re-elected and became the last provost before the councils of Blairgowrie and Rattray were united in 1928.

These worthies were workers at Ogilvy's Brewery which slaked local thirsts for several years. Bottles, or fragments of glass, from the brewery are still turning up, though not, alas, any of the tasty brew.

A scene outside the once busy Blairgowrie Railway Station. It stood on the branch line from Coupar Angus which closed to passengers in 1955. The line can still be traced for most of its route, although the bridge over the River Isla is no more.

Foreign gypsies, sometimes with a bear in tow, turned up in various parts of Scotland in the years before the First World War. This pair drew a crowd in Brown Street outside the dental surgery, now St Catharine's House, owned and run by the Episcopal church of that name next door. The house contains flats and meeting rooms.

A priest conducts a service from the steps of St Stephen's R. C. School. The worshippers are some of the Polish troops who were stationed in the town during the Second World War. Local people made many lasting friendships with their guests and the marriages that took place then and after the war has left the community with a colourful legacy of Polish surnames.

Ready for anything – members of Blairgowrie Home Guard on parade in the Wellmeadow, *c*.1943. The tall chimney belonged to the town's gas works and the gas manager occupied the house on the right, hence the name Gas Brae which is still in use.

For several years in the early 1930s, Blairgowrie Scouts went to summer camp at Easter Bleaton, Dalrulzion, with Scoutmaster A.M. ('Archie') Thomson who was also a high school teacher. These scenes show they enjoyed themselves, although one of the old boys remembers that the blanket-tossing had to stop soon after the picture was taken when the blanket tore down the middle!

Prizewinners at Blairgowrie High School in 1936. Standing from the left are Jim Ross, whose father was minister of the Barony Church, Alyth; Andrew Hoey, formerly of Glasgow; and Sandy Little from Clunie. The dux seated between the girls is Frank Davidson. The picture was taken behind the school which is now Hill Primary.

This was the youthful cast of an operetta performed in South Church Hall, *c*.1929. It was produced by Mrs More, wife of the then minister, the Rev. James More. For a small town, Blairgowrie has an impressive record in the fields of drama and music-making.

Hugh Grant and his delivery van were a familiar sight on the roads around Blairgowrie for many years. Here he is in the village of Meikleour in the 1930s.

The size of the Sunday School at St Mary's Church in the 1940s can be gauged by this picture of its team of teachers. Centre front is the Rev. James Leithead, the popular minister of St Mary's from 1929 to 1967.

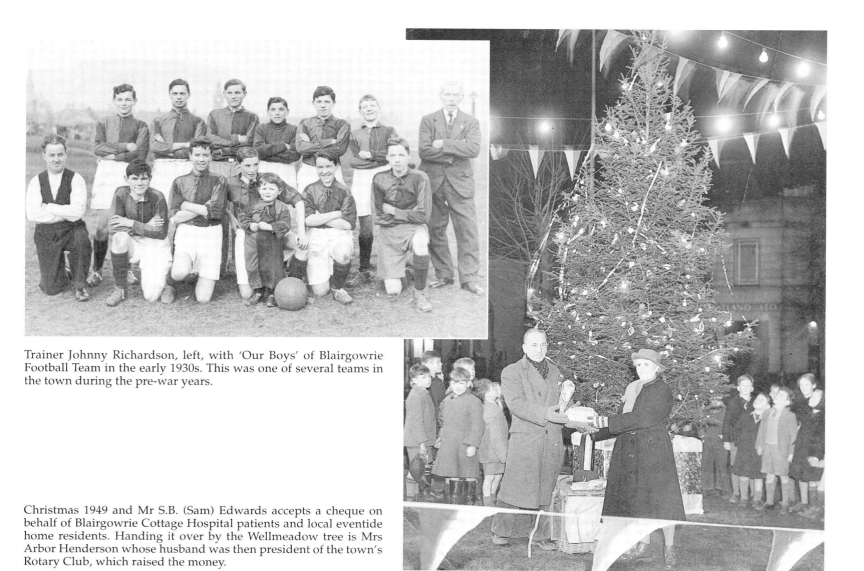

Trainer Johnny Richardson, left, with 'Our Boys' of Blairgowrie Football Team in the early 1930s. This was one of several teams in the town during the pre-war years.

Christmas 1949 and Mr S.B. (Sam) Edwards accepts a cheque on behalf of Blairgowrie Cottage Hospital patients and local eventide home residents. Handing it over by the Wellmeadow tree is Mrs Arbor Henderson whose husband was then president of the town's Rotary Club, which raised the money.

Three of the Ericht's once thriving textile mills can be glimpsed in this 1926 photograph. Westfield is on the left, while the roof of Brooklinn is on the right. The chimney of Ashbank is further down river on the right. Westfield Terrace, on the distant slope, was known as 'The Promised Land' when it went up. Its forty-eight houses were all occupied by mill workers and their families.

These young hopefuls casting their lines found a pleasant way to pass a summer afternoon on the Ericht. The old Craighall Bridge has long since been replaced, but anglers still cast for a trout or salmon on this stretch of the river outside Rattray.

A rare old view of the town's chief architectural treasure, Newton Castle. The oldest part is believed to date to the sixteenth century and it may stand on the site of an earlier stronghold. Two celebrated men were born here – George Drummond, one of Edinburgh's most notable Lord Provosts, and Thomas Graham, Lord Lynedoch, who won glory with Wellington.

Manse Court, on the corner of Upper Allan Street and Kirk Wynd, is named after this handsome old building seen here shortly before it was demolished in January 1989. The ivy-covered garden wall in the foreground remains, but the tall trees that overhung it and which were home to a large rookery also went in the redevelopment of the site. The Manse had become redundant on the closure of the Hill Kirk further up the brae.

This photograph of the standing stones on Essendy Road was taken in 1882. The fence seen here was put up in 1863 and was the first one on this stretch of the road. The circle was surveyed by an archaeologist in 1987 and the stones found to be in their original sockets. It is said to be the only group of standing stones in Scotland with a road running through them. They date from the Bronze Age or earlier.

Although on the extreme edge of Rattray, the parish kirk and Cross are very much at the heart of the community. It is sad, however, that it has been left without the interesting group of vernacular buildings seen here. They formed the perfect setting for the church, built in 1821, but were sacrificed in the interests of road improvements.

Later additions have altered the appearance of Rattray Primary School, although the original core of the building remains much the same as seen here early last century. Notice the absence of a fence between the playground and the Common. The field to the right of the school has disappeared under housing in recent years. The houses on the right, popularly known as 'the Connies', were built of mass concrete – the local belief is that they are too strong ever to be demolished!

Piper Frank Davidson leads the children of Marfield holiday home, Rattray, on their annual open day around 1933. Friends and supporters were invited to a tea party on the front lawn. Marfield later became the home of the well known Adamson family and is now a public house.

The postcard caption writer described these berry pickers as being 'at home' and, in a way, they were since there was probably temporary living accommodation for some of them in the farm buildings seen here. Hundreds of families used to come to 'the berries' from Dundee, Glasgow, Fife and further afield. Although the location in the photograph cannot positively be identified, the sheds bear a strong resemblance to those that lined Beeches Road when a farmer called Smith had berryfields there. The fields are now the site of Blairgowrie High School and sports field.

While the bigger fruit farms attracted city families and large numbers of travelling people to harvest the crops, smaller concerns like this one at Muirton of Ardblair usually depended on local pickers. This group are armed with their 'luggies' (small pails) for carrying in the 'drills', and the bigger buckets on the ground were for tipping the berries into. In time-honoured fashion, the small boy has his luggie hooked onto his belt. Nowadays the fruit is collected in coloured plastic baskets.

TELEGRAMS: DICK,
BLAIRGOWRIE.

BANKERS: NORTH OF SCOTLAND BANK LTD.

ESTABLISHED 1871.

TELEPHONE Nº 10.

Mr. R. Yeaman,
Burnbank,
Carsie.

JAMES DICK,
COAL, POTATO, MANURE &
FORAGE MERCHANT,
HAULAGE & CARTING CONTRACTOR.

ACCOUNTS QUARTERLY—
FEB. MAY. AUG. NOV.

Blairgowrie

Aug, 1936

		TONS	CWTS.	QRS.	RATE	£	s.	D.
1936	To Amt. of a/c rendd.					8	11	6
July 20	Haulage of 3 brls. Raspberries ex Carsie to Station.				6ᵈ		1	6
23 "	" " 3 brls do. do.				"		1	6
25 "	" " 7 brls. do. do.				"		3	6
28 "	" " 5 brls do. do.				"		2	6
30 "	" " 10 brls do. do.				"		5	-
						£ 9	5	6
Aug 1	Haulage of 4 brls. Raspberries ex Carsie to Station				6ᵈ		2	-
4 "	" " 7 brls. do. do.				"		3	6
5 "	" " 10 " do do				"		5	-
6 "	" " 4 " do. do.				"		2	-
					"		2	6
					"		-	6
					"		3	6
					"		2	-
					"		-	6
						£ 10	7	-

BLAIRGOWRIE,
31st Aug. 1936
Received Payment
£10:7:—
JAMES DICK
p. E & Wilson
WITH THANKS

A haulage bill from a local firm contracted to transport raspberry crops to the railway station at Blairgowrie.

This open air 'tinklers' waddin' at Muirton of Ardblair took place in 1910. On the left is the local minister, while the two witnesses, Geordie Boothroyd and Annie Murdoch, were both members of the little Muirton community.

According to the lady from Southport who wrote a message on this postcard in April 1951, she had just come over the Devil's Elbow and the snow at the roadside was eight feet high. Everybody in Blairgowrie and Rattray used to have a personal tale to tell about the dreaded hairpin bend which presented a severe test for early cars – and their drivers!

Visitors to the Spittal of Glenshee Hotel today would not recognise it from this picture taken before the fire which ravaged the building in 1966. Warm hospitality was dispensed here for many years by the Grant family. Long before that, the 'Spittal', or hospice, was a welcome stopping off place for travellers.

Heughs of Mause, Blairgowrie

The Heughs are the steep banks and gullies on the wooded slope running down to the Ericht between Woodhead Farm (or Tinkletap), top left, and Craighall Bridge round the river's bend. The twisting track in the foreground leads to Glasclune Castle and Muirton of Drumlochy. The path at the start of the once popular Heughs Walk can be clearly seen running along the edge of the field, centre, and then across the slope to the woods. It is presently badly overgrown.